Gentleman Jim

RAYMOND BRIGGS

GENTLEMEN

HAMISH HAMILTON

London

Other books by Raymond Briggs

THE MOTHER GOOSE TREASURY
THE FAIRY TALE TREASURY
*

THE ELEPHANT AND THE BAD BABY
text by Elfrida Vipont
*

FATHER CHRISTMAS
FATHER CHRISTMAS GOES ON HOLIDAY
FUNGUS THE BOGEYMAN
THE SNOWMAN
WHEN THE WIND BLOWS

Penguin Books Ltd, 27 Wrights Lane, London W8 5TZ (Publishing & Editorial)
and Harmondsworth, Middlesex, England (Distribution & Warehouse)
Viking Penguin Inc., 40 West 23rd Street, New York, New York 10010, U.S.A.
Penguin Books Australia Ltd, Ringwood, Victoria, Australia
Penguin Books Canada Limited, 2801 John Street, Markham Ontario, Canada L3R 1B4
Penguin Books (N.Z.) Ltd, 182-190 Wairau Road, Auckland 10, New Zealand

First published in Great Britain 1980 by
Hamish Hamilton Children's Books

This paperback edition first published in 1981
Reprinted in 1987
Copyright © Raymond Briggs

Printed in Great Britain by
Cambus Litho, Scotland

Gentleman Jim

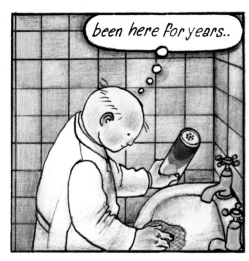

Time for a break...

...better look at the job opportunities...

Careers.... Let's see.. "Re-search-and Dev-el-op-ment Off-ic-er," mmm...

"Pro-duc-tion Direct-or"

Every BOYS Story Book | Out in the SILVER WEST | The BOYS Book of PIRATES | CAREERS in SURGERY | EXECUTIVE OPPORTUNITIES | The Monster Book For Boys | How to be a Diplomat

"Fi-nan-ci-al" Con-troll-er.

"Eur-op-ean-In-ter-nal Aud-it-Man-ag-er. Crumbs!

"Man-power-Train-ing and-Dev-el-op-ment Dir-ect-or- £18,000-plus-car" Crumbs! Triffic!

"ARE -YOU-A - DEC-IS-IVE-PER-SON?" No, s'pose not, really. Been thinking about Changing this job for 12 years

"BE-AN-OFF-IC-ER-IN-THE-ROY-AL-MAR-INES Man-y-car-eers-will-use-the-tal-ents-you-have- 'The-Nav-y-will-use-those-you-don't-even-know-you-have."

Crumbs! I wonder what talents I have what I don't even know I have?

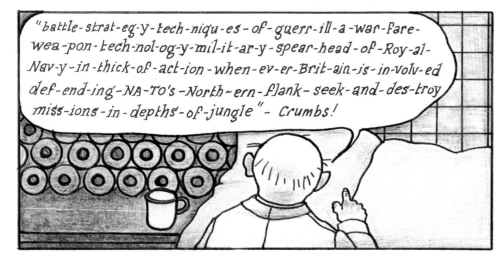

"battle-strat-eg-y-tech-niqu-es-of-guerr-ill-a-war-fare- wea-pon-tech-nol-og-y-mil-it-ar-y-spear-head-of-Roy-al- Nav-y-in-thick-of-act-ion-when-ev-er-Brit-ain-is-in-volv-ed def-end-ing-NA-TO's-North-ern-flank-seek-and-des-troy miss-ions-in-depths-of-jungle" - Crumbs!

Perhaps the Royal Marines Officers Course would unlock the key to my personality?

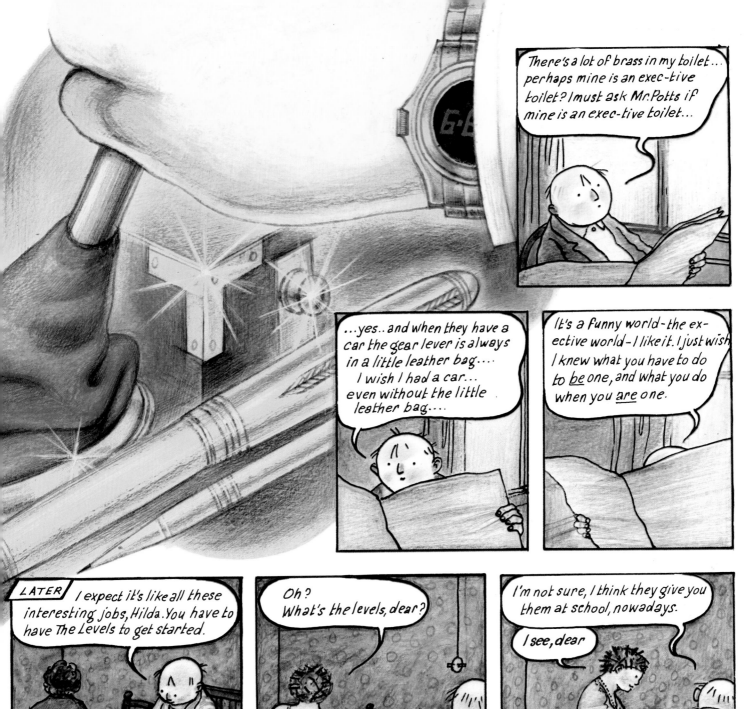

There's a lot of brass in my toilet... perhaps mine is an exec-tive toilet? I must ask Mr. Potts if mine is an exec-tive toilet...

...yes.. and when they have a car the gear lever is always in a little leather bag.... I wish I had a car... even without the little leather bag....

It's a funny world – the ex-ective world – I like it. I just wish I knew what you have to do to *be* one, and what you do when you *are* one.

LATER I expect it's like all these interesting jobs, Hilda. You have to have The Levels to get started.

Oh? What's the levels, dear?

I'm not sure, I think they give you them at school, nowadays.

I see, dear

They didn't give you any Levels did they, Hilda?

No, I don't think so, dear, They gave me a nice book, though.

Oh, what was it?

Prayers   Oh

"with a muffled oath, the two shadowy figures locked in mortal combat upon the parapet..."

"...but the room was empty! Nothing but a crystal goblet of wine stood upon the oaken table, a casement open to the cool night air, a billowing curtain...... then, from afar, they heard the distant thud of hooves and the faint echo of mocking laughter..."

Crumbs! This is great! This will take me out of the toilets.

"His keen, grey, aristocratic eyes scanned the distant horizon for the tell-tale dust cloud which would betoken the approach of the coach."

"With one bound, he leaped from the gallows tree onto the back of faithful Black Bess, and galloped away into the mist before the startled townsfolk could scarce draw breath."

Yes! This could be the answer! Be like Gentleman Jim – rob the rich and give to the poor! You don't need The Levels to be a Highwayman!

Hullo dear. Did you get our tickets to Texas?

Texas? Oh that! No dear. I want to get a sword.

I didn't think cowboys had swords, dear.

NO! Not cowboys! Highwaymen! Rob the rich and give to the poor. Gentleman Jim! The clash of steel on steel! Distant hoofbeats in the moonlit forest!

Goodness me! I didn't know they had forests in Texas, dear.

No! Not Texas! Cowboys are too expensive. You have to have an expert licence, a Cerstificate, a Customs Declamation, and all sorts of tripe. Besides, the boots are too dear.

Oh, I see. So I won't have the blonde wig and the fishnet tights, then?

No, my dearest.

Oh well, perhaps it would not have been suitable.

It was triffic expensive, dearest. The tickets were hundreds of pounds.

Ah well, I expect it's all for the best, love.

NEXT DAY

Ooh! There's a pistol! Real old one.

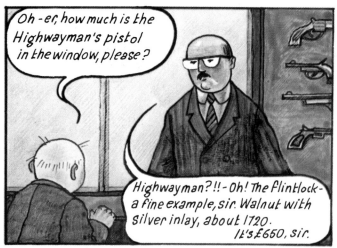

Oh - er, how much is the Highwayman's pistol in the window, please?

Highwayman?!! - Oh! The flintlock - a fine example, sir. Walnut with silver inlay, about 1720. It's £650, sir.

Crumbs! Have you got one a bit cheaper, please?

Yes sir, there's this small French one for only £320.

Oh - well, er...I meant.. ..about two or three pounds..

I should try a junk shop, sir.

Crumbs! Got to get a pistol. Can't be a highwayman without a pistol!

95p

DEAD-EYE DICK
PISTOL
You too can be a Marksman!

Dead-eye Dick.. ...Dick Turpin... perhaps that was the sort he had...

TOYS

Yes, I'll have one, please. Any swords?

Yes sir. This nice little rubber one. Guaranteed not to harm the kiddies - 50 pence

Mmm... I can put kitchen foil round it so's it will glint in the moonlight like cold steel...

FISHIN

BAIT
MAGGOTS
NOW IN

Crumbs! Look! Highwaymen's boots!

How much are the Highwayman's boots in the window, please?

Eh? Oh! The boots - the waders you mean. £4 chum. Second hand. In good nick - only a few small holes. Try 'em on

Pity they're not black.
You can always paint them - ha! ha!

Yes, that's an idea.

Hullo, I'd like to make enquiries with regard to the price of big black chargers...

Chargers – you know – horses...

For? Well... for riding on – and galloping through the night... and that...

A what? A gelding??? No, I wanted a horse

One thousand eight hundred pounds! Crumbs! I was thinking of about fifteen...

No, not fifteen hundred, Fifteen pounds...

Funny.... he's rung off... What's he mean – get a something donkey?

Could ask about donkeys, I suppose... not really ideal for the purpose... but when I get the first lot of gold...

Here we are... "Don-key-Sanc-tu-ary"

Hullo – I wish to make enquiries having regard to the price of donkeys.....

FREE! Crumbs! They're very old.. yes Need a good home...yes.. I see Will they gallop through the night?

I said "Will they..." Oh never mind, miss! I'll have one – black and glossy, if possible.....

Well, here she is, dear— Black Bess!

My Goodness! Is that the great black charger?

Well, it's the best I could do for the time being, my love.

We'd better put her in the back garden.

I wish we had a back entrance.

Are its feet clean?

Just a tick, dear. I'll put some newspapers down.

Ooh! My goodness! Look what's happened! Good job I put the papers down!

HEE! HAW! HEE! HAW!

The charger is making a terrible noise, dear. Perhaps it's hungry. Have you fed it?

No, I never thought. What does it eat?

Grass, I suppose.

Crumbs! Yes, it does! It's finished the lawn. I'd better take it up the Rec.

'Ullo, 'ullo, 'ullo! Wot 'ave we 'ere, eh?

Oh, it's my charger—Black Bess. Just giving her a feed.

A feed of Public Property, eh?

Well...just a bit of grass.

Just a bit of Public Property grass, eh? Muni-pical Corporation Sports Field grass, to be precise, eh?

Well, I thought...

Destruction of Muni-pical Corporation Sports Facil-ties, eh? The Public Parks and Open Spaces Act of 1887 don't make no mention of Commonland Grazing Rights, do it, eh?

Er....I'm sorry.. I didn't get The Levels... I don't know..

No. You don't know, but I do, Sonny Jim. Your animal is also Fouling the Muni-pical Public Footpath, and thus causing a Public Nuisance, innit eh? You'd better come with me to The Offices, my lad. I shall have to report this to the Muni-pical Authorities.

Crumbs! Authorities!

"I've left Black Bess outside for a bit...tied to a lamp post."

"You do look pale, dearest. Whatever's the matter?"

"Oh dear, I'd better sit down. I feel quite done up...all shaky... I got properly told off up the Rec. An Official spoke very severely to me. He's reported me to the Muni-pical Authorities."

"Never mind, love. Have a nice sit down and a nice cup of tea, then you can tell me all about it."

LATER

"Hullo! Knock at the door... I'll go...feel better now..."

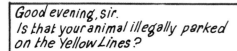

"Good evening, sir. Is that your animal illegally parked on the Yellow Lines?"

"Oh yes! It's my new charger Black Bess. I'm going to be a Highwayman!"

"I see, sir. Well, the animal has been illegally parked for 27 minutes within the area of a Restricted Zone..."

"So I must serve this Official Summons upon you and request you to remove said animal from the vicinity."

YOU, THE ACCUSED DO HEREBY SWEAR

"...but I live here..."

"I'm afraid that is entirely irrelevant, sir."

"Is it because of The Levels?"

"Beg pardon, sir?"

"Is it because I haven't got any of The Levels?"

"I'm afraid I'm not with you, sir."

"Could I leave her there if I'd got The Levels?"

"Sir! Not even an Official in Authority can Cause Obstruction on The Yellow Lines, sir!"

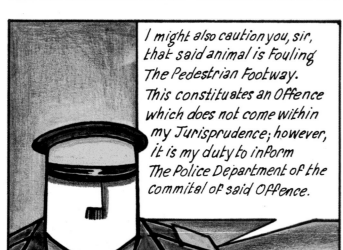

"I might also caution you, sir, that said animal is Fouling The Pedestrian Footway. This constitutes an Offence which does not come within my Jurisprudence; however, it is my duty to inform The Police Department of the commital of said Offence."

"Good evening, sir."

"Crumbs! .....commital...."

Who was that at the door, dear?

It was Someone in Authority. Another Official.

Oh my goodness!

They're after me before I've even started, Hilda. I expect it's due to modern security methods.

Oh dear!

What did he want, dear?

He's given me a Sums and he's going to commital me about the fence or something, he said.

I must keep Black Bess in the back garden, dear. Because the yellow lines are illegal.

Oh, I see, dear

NEXT DAY Good afternoon! Mr. Bloggs? Inspector Parker—jolly old R.S.P.C.A. We understand you are keeping a donkey here?

Yes, that's right. I'm going to be a Highwayman.

We've been informed that the jolly old donkey is insufficiently housed and inadequately fed. What?

No sir, not really sir...it's that at this moment in time I'm insufficiently organised at present, sir. I didn't know they eat all day, sir...

So the jolly old donkey is out in all jolly weathers? What?

Well, er...yes. Hilda won't have it in the house because of the — you know....

Well, Mr. Bloggs, I suggest you build a shelter for this jolly old donkey at once and see that it is fed and watered regularly....

...otherwise the jolly old R.S.P.C.A. will have to take jolly old legal proceedings against you. Is that jolly clear, what?

Yes, sir. Thank you, sir.

Good day!

Crumbs! Jolly old proceedings!

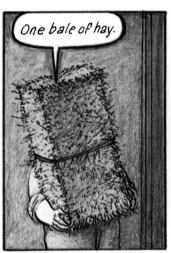

Mr. Bloggs? Good afternoon. Name – Morrison. Inspector – County Borough Council Local Urban District Offices – Surveyor's Dept. Understand structure erected back garden?

–Er – oh yes. The stable. The charger is nice and warm now, thank you, sir.

Volume of structure in excess of 66·373 cubic feet? Yes?

Er, feet? What feet?

Regret. Must inspect. Measure. Yes.

Hmmm.... Yes. Structure approximately 279·90751 cubic feet. Illegal. Yes Furthermore no record heretofore of Planning Permission Application at County Borough Council Local Urban District Offices Planning Applications Dept.

...Er...I'm sorry, sir. I couldn't quite... ...follow...

Ha–ve–you–app–lied–for– Plann–ing–Per–miss–ion?

Er..what's plied for planning permission? Is it to do with The Levels?

Structure contravenes County Borough Council Local Urban District Bye-Law Building Regulations. Must be dis-erected forthwith.

Dis-...?

TAKEN DOWN, MAN!

But I've only just erect it up. The Royal Society for Cruelty made me.

Necessary dis-erect immediately or Council forced prosecute. Heavy fine plus enforced dis-erection.

Regret prosecute. Nice horse. Good afternoon.

Crumbs! ... prosticute!!

Who was that, dear?

Another Official in Authority. He says I've got to take the stable down.

Oh, my goodness!

Yes, it's because of its feet, or something. He's going to prosticute me if I don't.

Oh dear!

The Cruelty Man is going to do Legal Proceedings to me if it's not up, and the Planning Man is going to prosticute me if it's not down.
Then there's the Muni-pical Authorities up the Rec. and the Sums from the Man in the Yellow Hat.

They've got The Law on me all round, Hilda. It's just like Gentleman Jim when the Bow Street Runners were after him.

The forces of Law and Order and Bow Street is closing all about me, Hilda.
The net is tightening. I wish I had a rapier of cold steel!

I wonder if the Man in the Yellow Hat is a Bow Street Runner?

Never mind, dear. You haven't done anything wrong have you?

Oh, no. Nothing. I'm a Free citizen and a Subject of Her Majesty. I'm innocent of all the preferred charges.

I'll be a quit in open court. They won't get me to yon gallows tree...

...but I'd better start robbing The Rich and giving to The Poor before they get me.

I'd better start this very night—er... i'faith!

Just going up to the bathroom to practice my silvery mocking laugh, for when I gallop away into the enshrouding darkness...

All right, my love. Don't be long—tea's nearly ready.

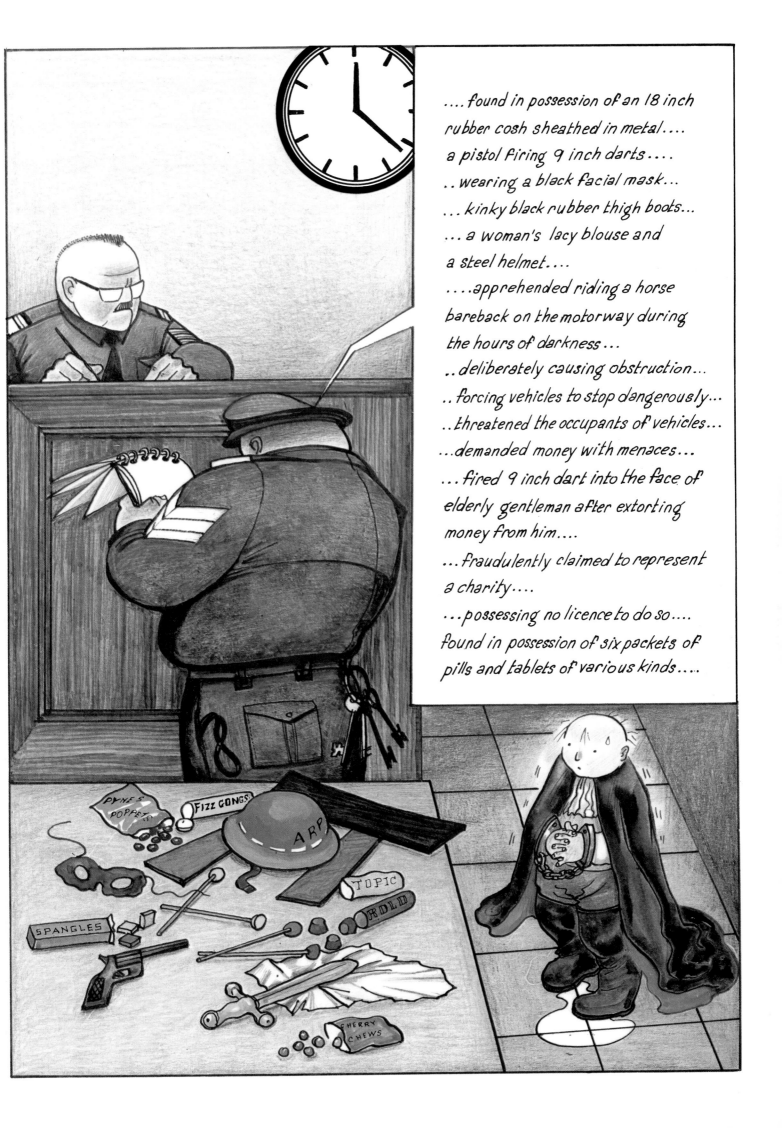

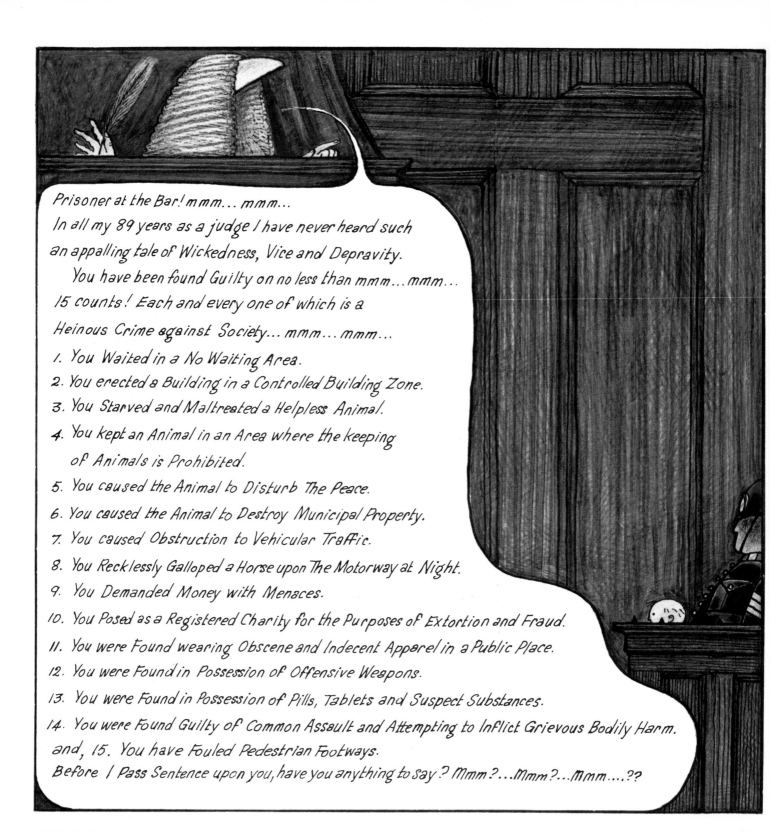

Prisoner at the Bar! mmm... mmm...
In all my 89 years as a judge I have never heard such an appalling tale of Wickedness, Vice and Depravity.
    You have been found Guilty on no less than mmm...mmm...
15 counts! Each and every one of which is a Heinous Crime against Society... mmm... mmm...

1. You Waited in a No Waiting Area.
2. You erected a Building in a Controlled Building Zone.
3. You Starved and Maltreated a Helpless Animal.
4. You kept an Animal in an Area where the keeping of Animals is Prohibited.
5. You caused the Animal to Disturb The Peace.
6. You caused the Animal to Destroy Municipal Property.
7. You caused Obstruction to Vehicular Traffic.
8. You Recklessly Galloped a Horse upon The Motorway at Night.
9. You Demanded Money with Menaces.
10. You Posed as a Registered Charity for the Purposes of Extortion and Fraud.
11. You were Found wearing Obscene and Indecent Apparel in a Public Place.
12. You were Found in Possession of Offensive Weapons.
13. You were Found in Possession of Pills, Tablets and Suspect Substances.
14. You were Found Guilty of Common Assault and Attempting to Inflict Grievous Bodily Harm.
and, 15. You have Fouled Pedestrian Footways.
Before I Pass Sentence upon you, have you anything to say? Mmm?...Mmm?...Mmm....??

...er...p..p..please, s...sir I..m...might have b..been..a..b.. better citizen if I'd had The L..L..Levels, sir...

What did you say?

WILL THE PRISONER PLEASE SPEAK UP!

..if I'd h..had L.. L..Levels, your Honours..

What is he saying for Heaven's Sake?

I'm afraid I've no idea, m'lud.

Dammit! It's nearly lunch time!

Then all that remains is for me...mmm to Pass Sentence upon you...mmm mm..bearing in mind your 37 years exemplary employment in-ah...er ...in...in your place of employment, I will be lenient with you...mmm...

..mm..so..er...I...mmm er...mmm..mmmm.....

I... I... the........Sentence of the Court.... upon you is That you Be Taken from This Place to an Awful Prison - er - Lawful Prison and thence to a PLACE of EXECUTION and That you There be HANGED BY THE NECK UNTIL YE BE DEAD!!!

M'LUD!!! M'LUD!!!

..oh..er..no... I...I....I'll... start again...

Heh! Heh! Those were the days!

Now...mmm..where was I ???.... Ah yes...mmm?...the sentence?... I sentence you to be detained During Her Majesty's Pleasure pending a Psychologist's Report..

Beg p'don, m'lud

Yes, what is it?

Not psychologist m'lud - psychiatrist

I said psychiatrist, dammit!

Yes, m'lud Of course m'lud Beg p'don m'lud

As I was saying...Her Majesty's Pleasure etcetera ....pending a psycho-thingummy's report ....take him away....

What's it like, dear?

Oh, it's not bad. It makes a change.

I've brought you a Robin Hood Annual and some Smarties.

Oh good, thanks. Triffic.

I might study for The Levels while I'm in here.

Oh, that's nice, dear.

Yes. I've found out I was right. They're only Education. There's Maths—that's like the sums we done at school, only modern. Then there's English—you know, spellin' an' that. And there's Modern Languages—sort of like the foreigners talk.

Oh nice, dear.

The Judge said it was for Her Majesty's Pleasure, didn't he?

Yes dear. Wasn't that nice?

Do they work you hard, love?

Oh no, it's cushy. They've put me on the toilets. They say I'm an expert.

Oooh! It's nice to be an expert.

Yes, it'll keep me hand in.

It's taught me a lesson, Hilda. I realise now I got ideas above my station.

Station. Yes, dear. I mustn't miss my train.

I hope I can get my old job back when I come out.

BRRRRINNG! TIME'S UP!

I hope so, dear.

Well, I'd better be off now. Goodbye, dear. God bless.

Goodbye, love.